I0756236

FINISHING LINE PRESS
www.finishinglinepress.com

Life Travels

poems by

Tina Harrach Denetclaw

Finishing Line Press
Georgetown, Kentucky

Life Travels

ISBN 979-8-89990-407-3 First Edition

ACKNOWLEDGMENTS

"Mother's Memory Book" first appeared in Silver Birch Press 'ALL ABOUT MY MOTHER' Series
"Sweet Arrows for the Heart" first appeared in *The RavensPerch*
"For the Love of Time" first appeared in *Verse-Virtual Journal of Poetry*
"Gingersnaps" first appeared in Silver Birch Press 'SPICES & SEASONINGS' Series on November 2, 2023. It was the author's first published poem.
"I Ordered a Storm Door Made in Minnesota" first appeared in *Synkroniciti Magazine*
"Celebrations" first appeared in Silver Birch Press' FAVORITE THINGS' Series
"Mile Marker in the Dark" first appeared in *Pulse: Voices from the Heart of Medicine*
"Favorite Shape" first appeared in *Verse-Virtual Journal of Poetry*
"Companions" first appeared in *Eclectica Magazine*
Photographs on pages 14 and 31 used with permission by Howard C. Martin
Image processing by Wilfred Denetclaw

Publisher: Leah Huete de Maines
Editor: Christen Kincaid
Cover Art: Philip Simon. https://philsimongallery.com
Author Photo: Wilfred Denetclaw
Cover Design: Elizabeth Maines McCleavy

Order online: www.finishinglinepress.com
also available on amazon.com

Author inquiries and mail orders:
Finishing Line Press
PO Box 1626
Georgetown, Kentucky 40324
USA

Contents

In Memory of my parents
and the family they brought with them

Dedicated to my husband
who is my first reader and favorite subject

With Thanks to my mentors,
Dr. Catharine Clark-Sayles and
Dr. Bertram G. Katzung

And for every teacher anywhere who has ever told a student,
You should do more of this

Sweet Arrows for the Heart

It was a private conversation
when my dad was giving praise.

Softly dancing words
under bushy eyebrows and glinting grey eyes,
almost a smile, head angled slightly,

he just barely leaned forward
                    to the lucky one.

I've seen the smiles back to him,
star-struck and grateful.

I have forgotten the words,
but I know the feeling.

When he taught me how to carry scissors safely
at three years old. When I mastered
my mother's bicycle at five.

What were his words that thrilled my whole
little self
with affirmation, the year before I started
Kindergarten?

They are hidden in the deep of my childhood mind.

But I still can hear
the gentle dance of his voice.

You talk to people so nicely.
My husband was pleased hearing me
compliment a waitress's work.

It is an easy grace.

I learned to do that at the best place on earth—
in the warmth of my father's praise.

The author's father

Smudge

In the winter night sky
facing south,

near to the horizon,
it's the smudge of light

just behind the scorpion,
steam rising from the teapot.

Sometimes I get lost driving
in my own neighborhood.

But I always know which way it is

to the center of our
Galaxy.

Henry and Esther

Go downstairs and get two cans of vegetables. Grandmother was making dinner for nine people. *What should I get?*

It doesn't matter. Just two of the same.

Grandma always had a butchered side of beef cached away in her deep freeze, and a wall filled with canned veggies in the basement—all bought on sale. She could start up a stalled truck as well as anyone. During WWII, Grandpa rebuilt engines for the Defense Department. Trash in a steel drum incinerator burst and burned him. He lay on a cot in the corner of their beadboard kitchen—for weeks—and described each step as his wife dismantled and rebuilt truck engines on the kitchen table. The same metal and dappled gray table where she had climbed and laid herself down to birth four children. Two decades later, a fifth was born in the hospital. Same doctor.

Grandma and Grandpa slept in a twin bed when they were first married—Henry and his tall, half-Irish bride. German with the looks of the Ottoman Empire, Henry's black hair was long and slicked back. A single jet eyebrow nearly crossed his forehead above his sapphire eyes. One grandson would have the same eyebrows. Esther's hair was black, too, from her German mother and wavy from her Irish father. Her eyes were hazel. She was poor growing up. Their only fruit, picked off trees down by the river in summer. They were evicted once. Henry courted Esther by helping her father load his horse-drawn wagon for hire. Esther's dog kept Henry out of her yard, regardless.

At 10 years old, Henry quit school to help his own dad work other people's farmland. After the Great War, he had his own trucks and he hired men. Some trucks carried sugar beets from fields to the refinery, other trucks carried manure from the stockyards to fields. He bought a one-bedroom house and, with his own hands, added two rooms to the back and put a basement underneath it. That basement was where Esther kept her canned goods. Esther stayed in school through eighth grade. She was winning a math contest when someone pushed her off the stage. I didn't know until Grandpa died that she had sewn all of his western work shirts, with styled yokes on front and back, and enameled snap fasteners down the front plackets. Smelling of grease and Lava Soap, they fit his shoulders perfectly.

Grandma threaded needles with both hands in the air. She licked the thread to a wet point, then thrid the needle's eye with confidence and precision. That's how Henry and Esther made their life together. Nothing certain, gaining what they could gather—with smarts and courage and exacting measure. One generation, from poverty to children with college degrees, and solid middle-class: a reverend, a teacher with her master's in reading, another teacher specialized in psychology, a concert pianist, a business owner. All taking on life with intention and calm grit.

Just get two of the same, Esther told me. And I did, like she did, and so did my mother.

Three granddaughters squeal
Grampa, Grampa, Grampa's home!
A young man takes a bride.

Henry and Esther

One More

Aunt Shirley's pecan pie, luscious
soft sweetness, crispy pecans
tenderly cradled in crust

Parents, siblings,
aunts, uncles, cousins sat—gathered
onto the couch, soft chairs,
hard chairs, the floor, or stood
wherever

scents of roasted meat
and cinnamon cake

wafted in air among them

laughter and teasing and storytelling
family with Grandma in her living room

Dad lifted his elbows, leaned back in his chair
and clasped his hands behind his head
His blue gray eyes smiling,
he told us—
Ohhh, that's good
Aunt Shirley's pecan pie.

Shirley perked across the room—*Do you want another slice?*

Dad signaled positive, spreading his hand in an upward motion
You bet! I thought it was all gone.

It is...
Shirley hurried from her seat
whirled 'round toward the kitchen—
her dress hem flying out behind her

This won't take long!

Shirley baked a whole new pie
because her sister's husband wanted

one more bite

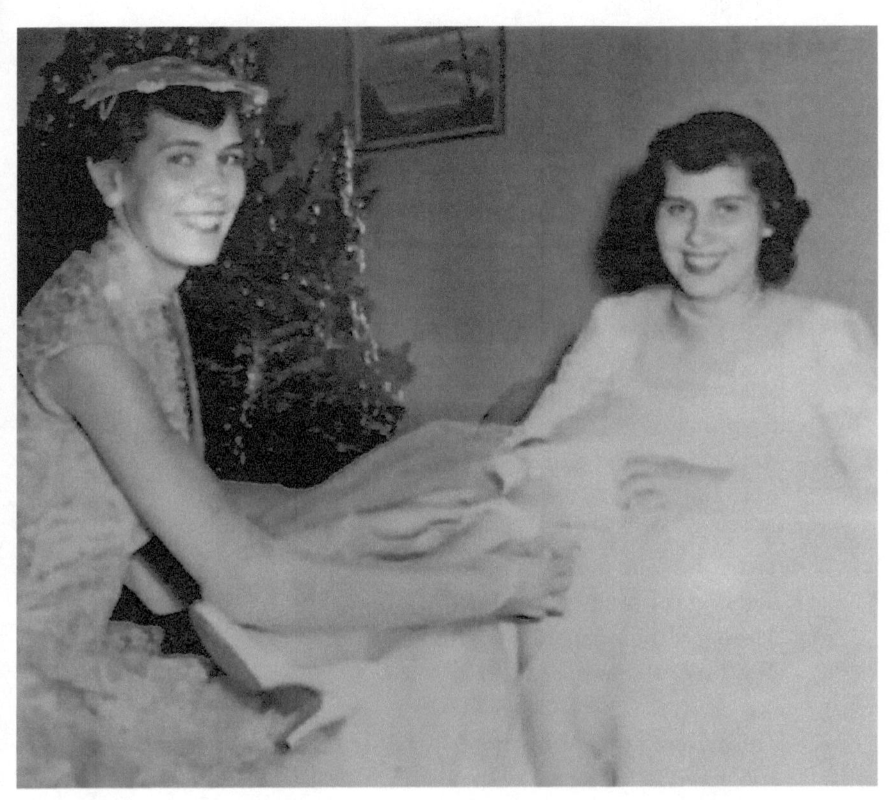

The author's mother on her wedding day with her sister, Aunt Shirley.

Mother's Memory Book

When my firstborn brother
flashed wet toddler grins,
his brown eyes glistened
with delight
and confidence.

He sat on the floor and pried open
five metal rings
in Mom's only cookbook—

the 1953 edition in red and white
gingham, her Better Homes and Gardens.
Its fluid line drawings scattered flair
amidst pages of text and measures.

His small fingers found skill
for punched hole papers and fastener
rings. He moved gathered pages
from one place to another.

There, he said, and snapped
five rings of binder closed.
Mom left those pages   where he put them.
That's where he thought they should be.

This tattered tome of grape jelly boulettes
and green jello salad
has passed into my home.

Browsing through

a time-capsule of food culture,
tender moments each time
I find a page out of

place.

Needlework

There's not enough tension on the bobbin.
Grandma lifted the presser foot, pulled fabric from under,
and showed me big loops on the backside. She turned the knob
for tension then showed me perfect stitches, top and bottom.

Early grade school, I stood next to Grandma's sewing machine
in the open room that Grandpa had built onto the back of the house.
A large plate glass window let in full light. Grandma made all of my
clothes when I was young, with fabric from the remnants bin.

Turquoise corduroys under a dark brown smock printed with
narrow blue lines—the Christmas before my second birthday.
A toe-headed toddler, I held Thumbelina, my baby doll,
in the bend of my arm as I tended a make-believe task.

Mid-teens, babysitting money bought me quality sweaters
off season on sale in a fancy ladies' shop, and I sewed my own
blue jeans. Years to come, I made Christmas dresses for my sister's
daughters—teddy bear prints under red pinafores.

This is a French knot. Aunt Shirley wrapped a tender woolen thread
around her needle twice, dipped into the white knitted blanket,
and made a coral rose. I was five and mesmerized. At fifteen, I filled
a chambray shirt with embroidered flowers before it was cliché.

It was my mother's hands that taught me crochet when my junior
high mind had other things to do. I stepped up for my generation's
grandchildren. Pumpkin hats and Christmas hats, and round white
caps for newborns—pink nipples at the back.

My favorite baby blanket—seven wide bands, light rose and soft mint,
made with the Jamie stitch. I watched my new-mother niece hold it up
to see, letting it rest on her out-stretched leg. My sister said—*Classic.*
Mom's wedding colors, Aunt Shirley's favorite stitch.

Like Mine

I sat on the polished stone steps in a central hall
and considered the hardboiled egg my mother cooked
for a field trip to the Museum of Pioneers.

Our teacher had set us loose to find what we might
in this history of where we lived.
I was surrounded by classmates whose families first
broke open the soil four generations ago.
Their parents were still making their life on the land.
Seeing and hearing excitement to explore their heritage,
I set myself apart.

My family rented a farmhouse and paddock in south central Nebraska.
Dad wanted his children to have horses, as he had hoped for when he
was a child. We were from somewhere else.

Two elderly ladies with coiffed white curls stopped briefly to say
kind words to me. They stroked my hair softly,
the same way my teacher did
as I waited for my fourth-grade picture to be taken.
They spoke to me as if I might know them.
I did not.

Solitary, I walked the rooms slowly—
studying the brown-hued photos of families,
sod houses, and sentry windmills
set tall on the expanse of plain,
a display of shoes, some colorful with raised soles
that kept skirt hems above the mud,
and handsewn dresses, some elaborate with bustle.
Farm tools were made of wood with rusted metal rings and blades.

Horizontal glass cases held silken embroidery, long flowing baby
gowns with pintucked bodices and tatted lace, spelling lessons
carefully drawn with chalk onto slate tablets.

A lush lock of hair tied with faded ribbon was set in a small wooden box
and placed under glass.
It was reddish gold,
like mine.

Fifty years later, I read that my great grandmother
immigrated as a child with her parents
from Denmark,
and settled in the next county over.

They were pioneers who broke open the soil
and made their new life from the land.

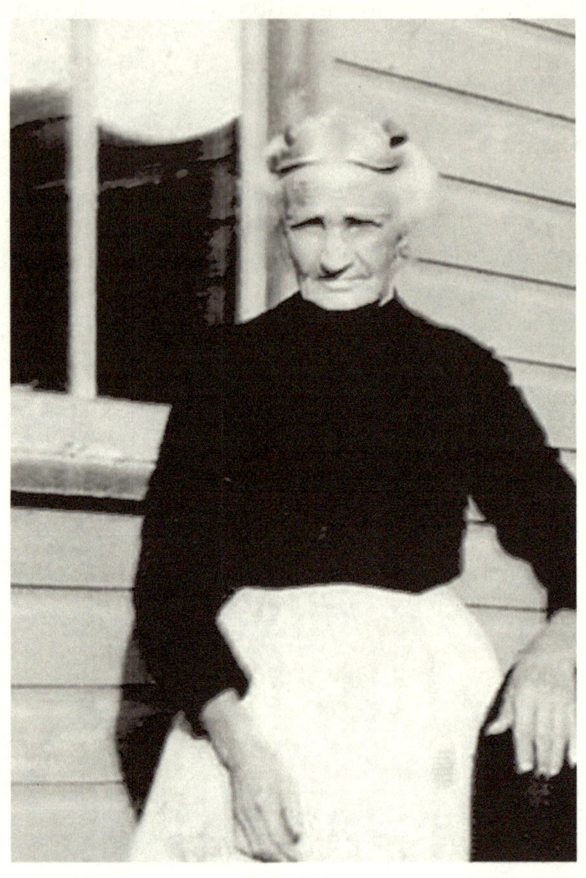

The author's great great grandmother, Caroline, in Rusco, Buffalo County, Nebraska, 1926. She immigrated from Denmark with her husband and children to south central Nebraska in 1893. Her daughter Nelsena, the author's great grandmother, later wrote for her local newspaper,
Farm Journal, *in Proctor, Colorado.*

Epigraph: The children in this poem lived in the rural area around Dannebrog, NE. This area was a mecca for Danish immigrants in the late 1800s and into the turn of the 20th century; Dannebrog is a romantic name for the Danish flag.

Debris

I think he came from Indiana. My aunt didn't know, you see.
Her grandfather's story was not all said, and so uncertain told.
A bit of nothing, dropped to ground, and left behind—debris.

A century of Appalachian kin, her great grandfather left Wythe County
before the Civil War. He went to Indiana, mustered with Union Corps.
My aunt never heard of this. She didn't know, you see.

His blue coat regiment chased General Hood to the waters of the Tennessee.
Veteran's pay bought a Hooser farm. He wed sweet Elsie, made a home.
A bit of romance, dropped to ground and left behind— debris.

Sons part grown, he ventured West to cut Nebraska sod. With Elsie
and their children, he brought old mountain talk along.
Appalachia carried to my aunt. She didn't know, you see.

My grandma spoke that way, I heard her, and my aunt, and cousin Connie.
In rural Colorado, their speech was different from anyone.
A bit of nothing, memories dropped and left behind so long ago—debris.

Was it an angry shun? Regret set too far back to speak?
Or was it accidental, not understanding how precious the telling?
Her name whispers Southern roots. Aunt Virginia never knew, you see.
A bit of lore unspoken. Dropped and left behind—debris.

Grandpa's Recliner

Black and white rough woven tweed
on its seat and half the back. Black leather headrest
and everywhere else.

That's where he sat as he cracked filbert nuts in
the evenings after each long day's work, or peanuts—
sitting on the floor all around him, grandchildren

smashing peanut shells, singing
the *Found a Peanut* song, and wondering
if a rotten peanut really could
send us to heaven early.

Pleased with our company
and his filberts, Grandpa was still in his vigorous
years, and ate nuts like

a young man does—handfuls at a time.

That chair followed me to college, always
a reminder of evenings with Grandpa
and my being born to play in his presence.

Moving day, my soon-to-be-husband picked up
the heavy recliner, turned it over, put it on his head
and walked out the door with it.

A bit astonished, Mother and I watched as the
young man who would become my husband
took on the world

like Grandpa did.

Gramma Saw Herself a Young Woman Walk in Through Her Door

I thought it was the flashing blue lightbulb
sitting in the silver cup
of Gramma's old camera.

She looked down into the lens box
and flashed to get each image.
So many strikes of light

each nauseating me
then making me
dizzy.

Flash again—
I cried out in my mind
I'm going to be sick!

I spent the next three days
with flu—Gramma didn't
know that

when I turned away from her
to let strobes of light fade
from my eyes.

Did you see your gramma following you?
My newlywed husband had seen.
She followed close behind you all night.

I didn't know.

For the Love of Time

On the roundabout in Kensington, there is a tiny shop
where the keeper's occupation is the cleaning and repair of clocks.
Our neighbor recommended him and so I ventured in
along with our wall ornament, a gift

from our cousin. The focus of our morning rush
fifteen years, now stopped.

I stepped into a clapboard store front, its tall windows lined with clocks,
found a bald-headed man wearing a leather apron,
and round glasses with no rims.

I laid our time-keep on his counter, and told him what was wrong.

It's plastic! his complaint.

But, it's been telling us we're running late for so very long.
He stopped a moment,
took a breath
then left—

He climbed a ladder in his closet, searching—his head and torso out of sight—returned with brush and oil in his pocket, then opened screws on our clock's back and lightly flicked a metal plate that hid corroded wires.

I'm sorry, this won't run.

And for a moment he grieved with me,
amidst the antique mantel clocks
that didn't have a home.

Moment

Sorting through apples
alone, missing my husband
Soft touch to my side

Moments

First glance I wondered
What is his future? him—he
liked my red sweater

Across the table
his gaze and words make me smile
My heart opens full

Laughter not guarded
I speak my mind, no filter
My thoughts safe with him

Dozing in our soft chair
a gentle presence brings my sweater
Sleepy memory

Sorting through apples
missing my husband—Surprised
his touch to my side

Life's arc still unknown
tender since we first began
Autumn's calm vespers

Gingersnaps

I've assembled a cooked sauerbraten marinade, spice-scented wine and root vegetables, now heating on the stove. The first time I made this recipe was in winter, 1982. It's from the book, *Great Dinners from LIFE.* Adjacent to the page with instructions for making sauerbraten, my copy has a cherry tart recipe with checks and conversions penciled onto the white space above the blocks of inked text. A set of parentheses was added within the text because instructions for the tart filling were given in the same paragraph as the crust and I kept needing to find the tart crust instructions. Evidence of a human hand, and therefore human experience, on a printed page. I feel a bit of an intruder when I see notes written in the margins of books owned by others. It seems that I have happened upon a personal moment, a handwritten intimate immortalized by connection to the printed page. This time, it was my own hand, and my own experience, and I was reminded of the hopes and feelings I had at that time in my life. Not yet graduated from college, but growing near; not yet engaged to the man who has become my husband of 44 years. Beginning to form a life, but still unsure of what that life would be. So much is known, now. So much is completed. And, a different set of unknown years lies ahead as I make this sauerbraten, again. Four days to soak, then brown and braise, then thicken the sauce with gingersnaps. My husband and I will have sauerbraten, and a few memories, for our dinner on Saturday.

I ordered a storm door
made in Minnesota

Maybe too much for our breezy weather,
but we do get wind-pounding rain

sometimes.

The gentleman who hung our door immigrated from Mexico.
He visited with my Navajo husband while I wrote his check.

They talked philosophy—peoples, culture, humanity.

Your house has a gentle spirit.
He was speaking to me.

It feels pleasant here.

My husband, home just two weeks after surgery
for an aggressive cancer.

There were surgical drains to milk and empty, wounds to dress,
protein shakes to make. Each task a quiet prayer—

grace seeding Grace.

I'd removed all turmoil from our life
like the radiant force of a newly lit star.

There is a different storm now, in the air and on the airwaves,
pelting us all.

I set my jaw and leveled my gaze as my father would do
in the face of danger.

You will not take the peace of our home.

And, I shut tight the solid new storm door

built to withstand a blizzard.

Celebrations

My third summer, 30 months old, sitting on a warm brick stoop.
Mother brought us ice pops, orange or red or blue,
sticky melt on hands and face, two wood sticks, two sides
each treat broken in half—one half for my brother, one
half for me. Then, one day for an unknown celebration,
both halves for each of us!

In my fifth winter, we arrived home in the dark, snow so deep and cold.
Daddy loaded three kiddos: one on his shoulders, one on each arm.
We laughed as Daddy navigated drifts to an icy sidewalk
and then   slipped—Whup, whup!
                                        He turned just right
and we all fell back into the snow,
no harm.   We laughed again.

One by one thru decades, shining stars of friendship
entered my life and never left, each one
a precious gift.

My husband and I never talked about politics or religion
before we married. As life proceeded with its challenges
and loss, we discovered a perfect fit. We grew closer
with each deeply felt find.

That ugly enemy my mother called The Big C,
Steve Jobs for all his money could not dispatch.
Now with a breakthrough combination
of drugs we already knew—high dose for tumor
still contained and removed, my husband just barely
met the rule—
a chance a chance a chance

and still a chance, these 30 months still clean.
Watchful waiting, a celebration each view
of markers normal, but first—courage
to open the tab and see.

My heavy heart breathes

thankful

for courage.

The author, far right, with her older brother and baby sister, on the stoop where ice pops were shared. Dresses made by Grandma. Photo by the author's mother.

Mile Marker in the Dark

Pancreatic cancer likes to come back early
if it is going to come back.

The longer it is gone the less chance you will see it again.
By two years, there is very little chance it will return.

The elderly doctor sat in for my husband's young radiation oncologist
and knew what we needed to hear.

Suddenly, we had a sign post.

We were grateful for the chance to live, but did not know
how long we would   hold   our breath
waiting for the unknown.

Already ten months
on a dark open road

stretching out in front of us
when that wise man showed us a mile marker.

And, now we are two weeks past that two-year signal.
We've not even a whisper from that deadly cancer.

Today, I smile softly, looking at my husband sitting in the car seat next to me.
He returns my gaze with grateful calm.

We have shut ourselves away from the world,
unable to abide cavalier unkindness or moments discarded
carelessly, as if they are soiled tissues.

And so, we will have dinner with my friend and her husband who is surviving
prostate cancer, and we will share together

quiet joy for the now
that we have.

Life travels

tossing bright pebbles
away from its wheels

what sticks in the tread
too often the burr
the broken edge
the smite

I wish I could forgive
as easily as my cat
who chastens me
then loves me
just the same, sees

all the bright pebbles
brings them to me

plays with my
shoe lace

Favorite Shape

Partial lines borrowed from Prometheus Unbound by Percy Bysshe Shelley, Act IV, Lines 519 - 521

Who doesn't love the golden spiral?
Measured progressions spun into strobiles,
sunflower faces and daffodil petals.

Pyramid triangles fall together
from a base of four sides.

Fractals bloom in a lighted screen,
Pachelbel's Canon in D.

If I must choose, I'll take the shape
of my husband's shoulders,
the gentle glide from his neck
to the round of his arm.

What is the math of a button-down
shirt? Skimming sinew and muscle,
set in soundless confidence
once noted by football rivals,
still owning the sidewalk,
now keeping me safe.

If math is required, then let it be
Shelley's divine sphere—

Beautiful orb!

Our Dearest, it must be you.

Thou, Earth, calm empire of a happy soul,
Sphere of divinest shapes and harmonies

Beautiful orb! gathering as thou dost roll
The love which paves thy path along the skies:

Prometheus Unbound by Percy Bysshe Shelley, first published in 1820; Act IV, Lines 519 - 522

The author's husband

Companions

The Sandhills of Nebraska
were once the bottom of an inland Sea

before blue Glaciers ground away
sturdy mountains to their ancient marrow
and let go their crushed debris onto
the dry basin

before young Rockies surged
the Seabed communed with living waters

Time presides through all
Over the arc of a day
the Sun retires
and draws long shadows into Dusk
then Night

Seasons pass

Millenia pass

silently

even the Sky is a distant
witness
to the slumber of unmeasured time

waiting

waiting

for the Ocean to return

The author's Gramma as a 4 year-old child (center) with her siblings and parents on their farm in Rusco, Buffalo County, Nebraska in 1910. The original homesteading two-room sod house, dug out from the side of a hill, still remained on the property at this time. Top left corner of this photo, the author's Gramma wrote, "Home Sweet Home" with double underlines.

Tina Denetclaw grew up in rural Nebraska and on the northeastern plains of Colorado where nearly all sides of her family immigrated in the 1800s as pioneering settlers. She has seen heart, determination, and intrepid courage passed down through the generations even when information about heritage did not. She slowly discovered more distant forebears through the internet and added their stories to what she learned from family who have been part of her life. Her closest and oldest friends are the children of farmers and ranchers. These relationships, in addition to her family, are key influences on her outlook and in her writing.

Denetclaw and her husband met in college freshman chemistry, married just prior to graduation, and came to Northern California for graduate school. Mountains on the east hand, ocean on the west hand, Redwoods and Tahoe, Monterey and Bodega Bays, Zellerbach and Shakespeare at Stinson Beach—Denetclaw was besotted. And so, she and her husband stayed and made their careers in their new home. Denetclaw is a clinical pharmacist, specialized in critical care and emergency medicine. Her husband is a biology professor. They have five cats and a large yard with a small orchard. The apple doesn't fall far from the tree.

www.ingramcontent.com/pod-product-compliance
Lightning Source LLC
LaVergne TN
LVHW090539110826
845146LV00003B/1184

* 9 7 9 8 8 9 9 9 0 4 0 7 3 *